This book belongs to

Name _____

Address _____

Date _____

A Look at the
Church of God

A Look at the Church of God

**the story of the church
for children
1930-1980**

by Merle D. Strege

**Published by
Warner Press, Inc.
Anderson, Indiana**

Copyright ©1989 by Warner Press, Inc.
ISBN 0-87162-599-7
All Rights Reserved
Printed in the United States of America
Warner Press, Inc.
Arlo F. Newell, Editor in Chief

Contents

Preface

Fifty years after the beginning of the Church of God movement, the people of this community had many reasons to celebrate. In the ten years from 1926 to 1935 the group's membership more than doubled, and people referred to the Church of God as the fastest growing religious group in the United States.* Church of God missionaries could be found on every continent. New boards and agencies gave oversight and leadership in important activities such as Christian education and youth work, home missions, and new church development. Anderson College and Theological Seminary had just entered its second decade of service to young people seeking higher education. New colleges were dreams in the hearts of several ministers.

With so much for which to be thankful and so much optimism about the future, men and women at the Gospel Trumpet Company set about planning the Golden Jubilee celebration. The Jubilee lifted up the accomplishments of the past fifty years and set the sights of the Church of God movement on the future. Plans were made to increase the number of people subscribing to the *Gospel Trumpet*. Money was raised to pay for the publication and distribution of new books such as Charles E. Brown's *A New Approach to Christian Unity*. A new hymnal *Hymns and Spiritual Songs* was published. The camp meeting of June, 1931 was to be a time of special spiritual refreshment and awakening.

Fifty years after the Golden Jubilee, men and women in the Church of God found new reasons for another celebration, this time giving thanks for one hundred years of faithful service and ministry. In 1980 Church of God people from around the world traveled to Anderson, Indiana, for the Centennial celebration at camp meeting and the World Conference of the Church of God. The number of people in the church had grown from just under 35,000 in 1928 to 175,000 in 1980. Sunday school enrollment in the United States had reached more than 280,000. In 1930 the movement possessed only one college, but by the Centennial six colleges had been founded as well as a graduate school of theology at Anderson.

New forms of ministry in radio and television had led to the creation of a Mass Communications Board. Women of the Church of God had begun its work of support for home and foreign missionaries and women. Church of God people could be found in nearly sixty countries around the world. The Church of God had also come to hold property in the United States and abroad valued at more than $388 million.

This volume tells in words and pictures some of the important stories about the Church of God in the years between the Golden Jubilee and the Centennial. Not all the stories that could have been told have been included here. The story of the Church of God is much too large to be included in a book of this size. Instead, I have chosen a few names and events out of the many that deserve to be remembered. Those whose names and faces you will find here represent dozens, or in many cases hundreds, of others. So it must be in any book that claims to be no more than an introduction. But if this book pricks the curiosity of its readers to go on to larger, more complete accounts of the history of the Church of God, then it will have accomplished one of its purposes, and not the least either.

---

*John W. V. Smith, *The Quest for Holiness and Unity* (Anderson, Ind.: Warner Press, 1980), 258.

Acknowledgements

Writing a book is not an easy project. It is a great deal more interesting, and a whole lot more fun, to read the words of these women and men you are researching, to collect stacks of photographs and imagine the kinds of persons they were whom you are studying. What captivated their hearts? What ideas fired their minds? Where had they traveled? What had they seen that impressed them?

Sooner or later, however, the writer of a book must take up pen and paper and begin writing. Then you discover how much you depend on the gracious cooperation of a whole host of people in order to get the thing done. It is only fitting that those people be acknowledged for their contributions to my work. Each one has added to what I have done. This book's shortcomings, and there are some, are my responsibility, not theirs.

First I want to thank the Archives of the Church of God, the Women of the Church of God, Warner Press, and the other agencies of the Church of God for the use of their photograph collections. Second, as she does with everything that I write, Joyce Krepshaw, faculty secretary at the School of Theology, clearly and accurately transformed my bad penmanship into words that people can read. Caroline Smith of the Warner Press Editorial Department, once again has edited my work with imagination, skill, and good judgment.

Finally, my wife, Fran Strege, collected many of the photographs reproduced here. To say that is not nearly enough, because the search for some of these photographs took her to some strange and uncomfortable locales. Not only because she worked hard to find pictures for my project, but because of her love for God, the church, and its children, this book is dedicated to her.

—MDS
Anderson, Indiana
Camp Meeting, 1989

Chapter 1: Home Missions

Jesus once said that nobody lights a lamp only to cover it so the light cannot spread. If you did not want the light to shine, why bother to light the lamp? Church of God people often spoke of their understanding of what God had done in Christ as "light" for them and for the church. This light was not meant to be covered but shared. Women and men of the Church of God movement sought to spread the light wherever they could carry it.

In 1921 a Church of God minister named M.F. Tafolla began a congregation among the Hispanic people of San Antonio, Texas. Reverend Tafolla was himself a Mexican-American. He learned about the Church of God through a copy of the *Gospel Trumpet* that he had received from a man named Ball. After Tafolla decided to become a part of the Church of God movement, Ball invited him to preach to the Mexican-American workers on his farm. This open-air preaching led to a Spanish language camp meeting on the Medina River near

Somerset, Texas. M.F. Tafolla began a congregation at San Antonio and pastored it for twenty-six years.

The year before Tafolla began his work in San Antonio, the General Ministerial Assembly of the Church of God created the Board of Church Extension and Home Missions. This Board was given two main assignments: (1) to establish new Church of God congregations and (2) to lend enough money to struggling congregations for building new church buildings. Russell Byrum served as the first president of this Board. He soon was replaced by Elver F. Adcock, who served the Board of Church Extension and Home Missions for many, many years.

One way the Board supported the planting of new congregations was

Pictured in the top photo are Marion and Eloise Tafolla. Members of the Spanish-American Concilio are pictured in the center. The lower photograph shows members of the Native American Council.

through the financial support of pastors. New congregations were too small to be able to pay their bills and a pastor's salary. As often as possible the Board of Church Extension and Home Missions offered assistance in such cases. Sometimes persons who received their financial assistance from the Board were called "home missionaries" as opposed to "foreign missionaries" who went overseas. M.F. Tafolla was the first Church of God home missionary who received assistance directly from the Board of Church Extension and Home Missions.

Hispanic congregations began in other Texas cities and towns. Tafolla's work in San Antonio and his camp meeting on the Medina led to the founding of a congregation in Somerset shortly after the beginning of the San Antonio church. L.Y. Janes started a Hispanic congregation in Corpus Christi in 1933. Janes wanted to spread word of the Church of God movement through the written as well as the spoken word. So he started the Christian Triumph Publishing Company. This organization published *La*

Trompeta, the Spanish language *Gospel Trumpet*, until the 1970s. The Corpus Christi congregation began a second church in that city. Although its name at first was the "Spanish Mission," eventually, under the leadership of Lorenzo Ramos, it took the name *"La Iglesia de Dios"*—The Church of God. Evangelistic efforts by these congregations also reached out to places like Refugio, McAllen, and San Benito. The Corpus Christi congregation started churches as far away as Albuquerque, New Mexico, where Amelia Valdez began organizing Bible schools in 1952.

Home missionaries were also very active among Spanish-speaking people in southern California. In 1920 Church of God people organized the Spanish Evangelical Association. This organization published a monthly paper, *La Verdad Apostolica (The Apostolic Truth)*. Although the association was located in Anderson, it helped begin a congregation in Los Angeles. In 1931 Reverend A.T. Maciel started a congregation there. He served the Los Angeles congregation (known as

Belvedere Church of God) until 1950. In 1937 the Board of Church Extension and Home Missions helped bring about the congregation's dream of being able to worship in their own church building.

After Reverend Maciel left Belvedere church for missionary work in Mexico, the congregation was served by others such as Maurice Caldwell and Samuel Colunga. In 1959 Fidel Zamorano began pastoring the Belvedere church. In addition to serving as pastor, Reverend Zamorano has been speaker on *"La Hora de Hermandad Christiana,"* the Spanish language version of the Christian Brotherhood Hour.

Spanish-speaking peoples have come to the United States in ever-growing numbers. The Church of God movement has attempted to enlarge its work among these people as they spread throughout the country. In 1968 the National Memorial Church of God in Washington, D.C. began sharing its building with a Cuban congregation pastored by Roberto Oliva. Cuban congregations led by Ellsworth Palmer and

Antonio Grizzell began in the 1970s in Miami. Phoenix, San Francisco, Denver, and Toledo all had Church of God Hispanic ministries in the 1970s. Many other congregations have been started in Texas and California as well.

The Spanish-speaking congregations thought that fellowship with one another was important and something that they were missing. They also thought they needed an organization that would help them plan for the growth and development of their established churches as well as the new ones they would start. In 1954 they organized the Spanish-American *Concilio* of the Church of God to help them meet these aims. The *Concilio* also is concerned with the education and training of future Hispanic Church of God leaders. The Board of Church Extension and Home Missions cooperates with the *Concilio* in the effort to achieve these goals.

Both buildings shown here are chapels at Wounded Knee on the Pine Ridge Indian Reservation in South Dakota. The top photo shows the new chapel, which replaced the one shown below it. The Board of Church Extension and Home Missions helps finance the construction of many buildings such as these.

Native Americans

Home missionary work among native Americans began on two different reservations in March of 1939. J. Frank Shaw was pastor of the Church of God in Everett, Washington, north of Seattle. The Tulalip Reservation was very close to Everett, and one of the members of Shaw's congregation, Rollo Maulsby, leased some of the reservation land. Maulsby invited Shaw to the reservation, where he could see the needs of the people for himself. The reservation Indians had been treated badly, and Shaw's heart was deeply touched when he saw their physical and spiritual needs. Right then he determined to begin a mission among the Tulalip Reservation Indians. Progress was slow, but Mr. and Mrs. Shaw always made sure that the Indians were invited to their salmon bakes and Christmas programs. After a while a congregation began to grow.

In 1943 the Shaws moved to Toppenish, Washington to begin another native American church. Adam and Marge Williams replaced them at Tulalip. Mr. Williams was a Swinomish Indian who had graduated from Pacific Bible College in Portland. He continued as pastor of the Tulalip congregation until his death in 1978. Marge Williams also was a pastor of the congregation, and she continued their work at Tulalip after her husband's death. The Williams carried the gospel to those who lived on the reservation. This gospel brought healing of spiritual, emotional, and physical needs. Adam and Marge Williams had a special concern for native Americans suffering from alcoholism, and they worked particularly among them.

At the same time that the Shaws started their work at Tulalip, another native American Church of God congregation began on the Pine Ridge Reservation in South Dakota. Some students from Gordon, Nebraska, held worship services in the home of a Sioux Indian named Robert Fast Horse. They were asked to return, and so a small gathering began in the midst of the awful despair and terrible conditions of Pine Ridge. The massacre of Indians at Wounded Knee on December 29, 1890 was only one of the many sad stories that the Sioux people of Pine Ridge could tell. But Church of God home missionaries began bringing words of hope and encouragement to those who had known such terrible suffering.

The first Church of God congregation on Pine Ridge Reservation was located at Wounded Knee. In 1973 this town was occupied by members of the American Indian Movement. Some people wondered whether this meant the end of the Church of God at Wounded Knee. But the congregation survived and continues to offer spiritual hope and material goods to the Sioux of that district.

As Indians have moved off the reservations Church of God people have tried to meet their physical and spiritual needs in towns and cities where the Indians have located. So special projects, sponsored in part by the Board of Church Extension and Home Missions, have begun in places such as Gordon, Alliance,

These four men served as leaders of the Board of Church Extension and Home Missions from its beginning through 1980. They are Elver Adcock (upper left), Russell Byrum (upper right), William E. Reed (lower left), and Marvin Hartman.

and Scottsbluff in Nebraska and Park Hill, Oklahoma. Other home mission projects can be found among the Nez Perce at Lapwai, Idaho; the Crow Indians at Crow Agency, Montana, and the Navajo at Klagetoh, Arizona. In 1979 the Church of God opened a mission among Alaskan native Americans and Eskimos through the ministry of Fred and Evelyn Mamaloff.

The Board of Church Extension and Home Missions has sponsored many different projects in North America. All of these projects aim at spreading the gospel. Sometimes these projects require money, and then the Board acts like a bank, loaning dollars for church construction. But the Board also uses money to support projects such as those among the Hispanics and Native Americans. It also sponsors projects in some of America's large cities. Wherever the project, whatever its kind, the Board of Church Extension and Home Missions seeks to spread the Good News of what God has done. □

Since its early days, people of the Church of God movement have felt the importance of traveling throughout the world to tell men and women and boys and girls about the life-giving power of the gospel. Those whom we call *missionaries* often sacrificed many of the comforts we take for granted. They left the familiar customs and surroundings of their homeland and often had to learn new ways of understanding. Missionaries nearly always left friends and some family members behind. They risked serious illness and sometimes their own safety for the sake of the gospel.

By 1930 missionaries of the Church of God had spread around the world. Mr. and Mrs. William Hunnex had begun a mission at Chinkiang, China. The *Australian Gospel Trumpet* was started in Sidney by E.P. May. Missionaries had opened a station in what now is known as Lebanon. Missionaries also established congregations in Caribbean islands such as

Chapter 2:
Missions and Missionaries

Jamaica, Barbados, and Trinidad. They carried the message of the gospel and a vision of the Church where all Christians worship as one great family.

The Church of God in Kenya

One of the largest Church of God missions anywhere in the world is in Kenya. Dozens of men and women have served as missionaries in this part of eastern Africa. You will see that their story is an exciting example of the gospel's growth among the tribes of that region.

In 1917 the Misssionary Committee of the Church of God commissioned the Samuel Joiners and the William Baileys as missionaries to Kenya. But even before they left the United States, the Church of God had established a Kenyan mission.

Missionaries Mabel Baker, Henry and Gertrude Kramer, and Mabel's father, A.W. Baker, had been proclaiming the gospel in southern and eastern Africa many years before Church of God missionaries arrived. Mr. Baker established a mission in the western province of

Kenya on land given to him by Chief Otieno of Bunyore. Mr. and Mrs. Robert Wilson opened the mission and named the station "Kima." Not long afterward Mabel Baker and the Kramers arrived and the mission work grew. They learned tribal languages and translated parts of the Bible so that the tribespeople could hear the gospel read and spoken in their own language. Schools opened for the children.

Along with the Wilsons, a young man of the Zulu tribe named Johanna Bila traveled to Kima station. Johanna had just recently become a Christian. At Kima he witnessed to the love of Jesus and God's power to make people whole.

The story is told that Johanna planted a garden of peanut plants. But as the peanuts ripened his neighbors would steal them from his garden. Johanna did not complain about their stealing. He just kept planting new peanuts. His patient love for his neighbors continued in this manner until the day he died.

In 1921, while visiting in Pomona, California, the Kramers met Abram and William Bixler, two brothers who told their new friends about the Church of God movement and its hope that all Christians could be one. The Kramers believed in such a church and decided to join in the same cause. But they also longed to return to Kenya and continue their missionary work. After sending people to inspect the Kramer's mission, the missionary committee agreed to take over the support of the Kima station as a Church of God mission. In 1922 they appointed Henry and Gertrude Kramer as missionaries of the Church of God.

Others joined the Kramers in Kenya after their return. The Baileys went to Ingotse as agricultural missionaries in 1924. Ruth Fisher joined the mission as a teacher for the missionaries' children. She married another missionary, James Murray, in 1925 and together they worked in the boys' school which began at Kima and then moved to Ingotse. In 1927 John and Twyla Ludwig arrived at Kima, where Twyla began a girls' school.

Soon churches began as the gospel spread. They could be found in villages and towns like Kisii, Kakamega, and Butsotso. A young man named Musa Eshipiri heard the gospel and believed on the Lord Jesus Christ. He gave some land that he owned to the missionaries for their work. They soon started a new mission at Mwihila on Musa's land. Homer and Vivian Bailey opened this station, and in 1939 Jewell Hall, a nurse, opened a clinic there.

Miss Hall's clinic illustrates an important part of the Church of God mission in Kenya. Women missionaries often began medical treatment at their stations with whatever medicine and equipment they had.

Twyla Ludwig opened a larger clinic at Kima in 1928. This grew into Kima Hospital. In the same way the clinic started by Jewell Hall at Mwihila also expanded and offered more services to the tribespeople of the area. It, too, became a hospital. Of course, hospitals need doctors and nurses to staff them. Church of God missions hospitals have been well served by doctors such as David Gaulke, the first

missionary doctor in the Church of God, and William Anderson. A few of the names of missionary nurses who served in Kenya from 1930 to 1950 include Irene Engst, Jane Ryan, Elsie Gaulke, Rosa Bollmeyer, and Edna Thimes. These are only a few of the many others who could also be named.

Life was hard in the early days of the Kenya mission. Travel and communication were difficult. Robert Wilson traveled on foot or bicycle to many of the villages and towns where he witnessed to God's saving power. Missionaries also risked serious illness. Ruth Fisher Murray died of typhoid fever in 1936. Four years later her husband,

Egyptian members of the Church of God movement, pictured above, benefitted from the missionary work of many women and men especially after World War II. Below are pictured John and Pearl Crose and their sons Lester and Kenneth. This family served the missionary work in the Mediterranean area and elsewhere for two generations.

James, died of a deadly form of malaria called blackwater fever. The Murrays had three children, all of whom died as infants. The Murray family is buried at Kima cemetery. Today at Ingotse stands Murray Memorial Chapel, dedicated to the memory of their sacrificial service.

The Church of God on Mediterranean Shores

The Nile River flows north out of east central Africa to the Mediterranean Sea. Kenya lies at one end of this great river, and Egypt lies at the other. Church of God literature circulated at Port Said, Egypt before 1900 when Gorham Tufts spent a month there on his return from a missionary trip to India.

Until 1923 Church of God missions in this Muslim land were conducted by G.K. Ouzounian in Alexandria and Mossad Armanious in Assiut. Occasionally short-term missionary-visitors came for as long as seven months, as E.A. Reardon, George Tasker, and Hiram Brooks did in 1907. The first regularly appointed Church of God missionaries to Egypt were Thaddeus and Katrina Neff, who arrived at Port Said in 1923. For the next ten years the Egyptian mission grew rapidly. Salib Farag, an Egyptian Christian, took charge of the publication of *Buk-el-ngeel*, the *Gospel Trumpet* in Arabic. The William Fleenor family joined the mission in 1932 while Nellie Laughlin served there twice, 1929-31 and again from 1937 to 1942.

The Egyptian mission was only part of a vigorous Church of God missionary effort in the eastern Mediterranean. The other main arena of activity was in Syria—now known as Lebanon. Missionaries to this area included H.M. and Minnie Riggle and veteran missionaries John D. and Pearl Crose. Their sons, Lester and Kenneth, along with their wives, Ruthe and Mabel, continued their parents' work in the Middle East. Church buildings were erected in Beirut and Tripoli. Ibrahim Maloof carried the gospel of Jesus to villages in the farther northern districts.

World War II slowed the expansion of Church of God missions in the Mediterranean as elsewhere. But the war's end brought a renewed effort to expand the work of the church. Wilbur and Evelyn Skaggs joined the Egypt missionary staff in 1945. Nicholas and Rose Zazanis returned after the war, as did the Neffs and William Fleenor. The congregation in the Shoubra district of Cairo acquired a church building and parsonage. Youth centers were established in Cairo and Alexandria. In the 1950s Ernest and Grace LaFont and C. Jean and Ruth Kilmer joined the missionary staff. The Church of God mission in Egypt had entered a time of real development and growth.

The stories of Church of God missions in Kenya and Egypt could be repeated in many places around the world. New mission stations were begun, and established ones grew larger on many of the islands of the Caribbean and the nations of South and Central America. When the Communist revolution reached China, Church of God missionaries were forced to leave a flourishing mission, though some of that work has miraculously survived to the present time. Other works expanded in Hong Kong in the aftermath. In

Children have been especially important to Church of God missionaries. That is why schools have been part of the church's missionary work. Children in Guyana [formerly British Guiana] must carry water home from the well. But they also were given the opportunity to learn in one of the mission schools operated there by the Church of God.

Two leaders of the Missionary Board of the Church of God, Lester Crose (left) and Donald Johnson.

countries around the world you still hear stories told of devotion and sacrifice by Church of God missionaries who answered the call to spread the gospel. ☐

The photographs on this page were taken in Japan, where Church of God missionaries have been active since 1911. Schools have been important parts of the missionary work there, as in other parts of the world. In the lower photo Arthur and Norma Eikamp, who went to Japan in 1949, are shown with the 1957 graduating class of the Tamagawa church kindergarten.

Women have played important roles in the work of the Church of God from its very beginning. They preached, they organized Sunday schools, they taught, they worked in the Gospel Trumpet family. At an especially critical time in the movement's history, Church of God women stepped forward to spread the gospel in a new way. They created an organization that directly supported the missionary work of the church. Through the years that organization has given women the opportunity to grow as servant-leaders in the Church of God movement and beyond.

By the year 1930 Church of God missionaries were spreading the Good News of salvation all around the world. They served in Egypt and Syria, India and Japan, Barbados and Trinidad. People in the United States and Canada gave money to the Missionary Board, which used that money to pay missionaries their salaries. (Then they were called allowances.) Missionary allowances were never very high, but in 1926 and again in 1928

Chapter 3:
Women of the Church of God

their allowances were reduced because not enough money was being given for missionary support.

Just as missionary allowances were being cut, some even worse news came. The Great Depression began in October, 1929. Millions of people lost their jobs. They no longer had money to give to missions or any other cause. The Missionary Board had to cut allowances again, but the missionaries remained at their work.

About the same time that the depression began, a Church of God minister named Nora Hunter traveled to Egypt and Lebanon to visit the church's missionary work there. Pastor Hunter had been a minister for more than thirty-five years. She had known D.S. Warner and other early leaders of

Nora Hunter, top photo, was the principal leader of the National Women's Home and Foreign Missionary Society and its first president. Shown in the lower photo is the national board of the society in 1937.

the Church of God movement. After visiting the missionaries Pastor Hunter became deeply troubled. She grew more and more unhappy that their already slender allowances were being cut more. She was also sorry that the Missionary Board could not send more missionaries to other places in the world where people had not heard about Jesus. She returned to America determined to change things.

At Anderson Camp Meeting in 1931 Nora Hunter talked with other women about the needs of missionaries and the church's need to send more missionaries. They agreed with her and together they asked the Missionary Board if they could help solve the problem of

In 1938 Friends of Mission *was produced in the home of Hallie Patterson (standing, left). Four women leaders in the Church of God shown (center) are Axchie Bolitho, Esther Boyer, Mae McAlpine and Nora Hunter. The lower photo pictures brunch at the 1977 convention of the Women of the Church of God.*

finding money for the missionary work of the church.

Along with Nora Hunter, Mrs. E.E. Byrum, Mrs. T.A. Berry, and Olive Sheefel planned ways that women of the Church of God might organize across the nation to raise money needed to keep missionaries at their stations around the world. In 1932 their organization was approved and became known as the Women's Home and Foreign Missionary Society. Nora Hunter was its first president, and she served in that position for sixteen years.

Immediately Nora Hunter began crisscrossing the United States in behalf of missionaries. Her slogan was "full allowances for our missionaries and help for our national workers." She organized countless women's missionary socie-

Presidents of the Women of the Church of God have included Betty Lewis (top), Helen Miller (center, left) and Nellie Snowden (center, right). Snowden also served as Executive Secretary-Treasurer, as did Hallie Patterson (below).

God so loved the world, that he gave his only begotten Son, that whosoever believeth in him should not perish but have everlasting life.

—John 3:16.

Jesus Commanded:—Go ye into all the world, and preach the Gospel to every creature.

—Mark 16:17.

This is love, that we walk after his commandments.

—II John 6.

Freely ye have received, freely give.

—Matt. 10:8.

Make it a habit to place daily a penny or more in the envelope below — God will reward you. Once a month remove the envelope and give to your local missionary society treasurer. Money collected through the use of this calendar will go to the missionaries.

CONSECRATION

*Take my life and let it be
Consecrated, Lord, to
thee;
Take my hands, and let
them move
At the impulse of thy
love.*

*Take my lips and let them
be
Filled with messages
from thee;
Take my silver and my
gold;
Not a mite would I
withhold.*

*Take my moments and my
days,
Let them flow in end-
less praise;
Take my intellect, and use
Ev'ry pow'r as thou
shalt choose.*

*Take my love, my Lord, I
pour
At thy feet its treasure-
store;
Take myself, and I will be
Ever, only, all for thee.*

—Frances R. Havergal.

"Other sheep I have, which are not of this fold: them also I must bring."   —John 10:16.

WOMEN'S HOME AND FOREIGN MISSIONARY SOCIETY
CHURCH OF GOD

*A Daily Gift, A Daily Prayer,
That All The World Our Christ May Share*

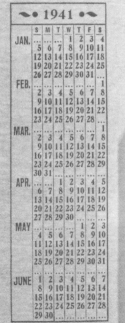

Shown here is the women's society's Penny-a-Day calendar for 1941. Each day the owner of such a calendar was to put a penny in the envelope and pray for the church's missionary work.

ties in local congregations and helped develop state organizations, too. She wrote a monthly *President's Letter* which eventually led to the publication of a society magazine called *Friends of Missions*. In 1951 its name was changed to *Church of God Missions*, the name by which it is known today.

As the young society swung into motion, women began projects that would raise money for missions. They cooked and baked, they knitted and crocheted and sewed. The goods they made with their own hands they then sold, and the money they earned went to missions. They also saved pennies. In 1935 the women's missionary society began distributing "Penny-a-Day" calendars to its members. The idea was simple. Save one penny and say one prayer for missions every day of the year: "A penny a day while you pray." If one thousand women saved a penny a day, the society would have $3,650 to give to missionaries. That may not seem like much money by today's standards. But in 1938 $3,650 could pay the allowances of seven or

eight missionaries.

Because of the dedicated hard work of the members of the missionary society, not one single missionary had to be recalled from his or her assignment. In 1934 the Missionary Board acknowledged the immense service women had made to the missionary work of the church.

Through the years the women's organization has grown. Its name has changed as well. Today it is known as Women of the Church of God. The women's organization has raised and donated money for many worthy projects throughout the Church of God movement. The women's organization has donated money for some of our church college libraries, ministers' pensions, scholarships, and church buildings in Nairobi, Mexico City, and other places around the world.

By 1981 the organization had raised a total of $20 million for church projects. But this does not include tons of clothing as well as food, medicine, and other supplies sent overseas by the Women of the Church of God.

The Church of God women's organization over the years has enlarged its mission. It has taken on more projects than raising money for home and foreign missions. The organization is concerned about developing leadership skills among women and for years has offered courses in those areas. More recently the Women of the Church of God has stressed the point that "its programming was for women with their needs, interests and contributions in mind."* They have raised the awareness of many concerning the value of women throughout the

*Hazel Neal and Axchie A. Bolitho, *Madam President: The Story of Nora Hunter*, revised by Marie Meyer (Anderson: Warner Press, 1982), 116.

world in many places where women are seen as unimportant. In these ways and more the women's organization has fulfilled the vision of Nora Hunter, who saw more clearly than anyone else the creative power and strength of the women of the Church of God: □

Ocie G. Perry, President of Women of the Church of God from 1948 to 1960.

Radios and televisions are things that today's children learn about from their earliest years. But in the 1920s, long before television was ever invented, Americans were just beginning to use a wonderful new invention—the radio. Families tuned in to hear news reports and entertaining programs. In the 1930s Church of God pastors began radio programs on local stations. Since people were using the radio to broadcast news, weather, and sports, why not use it to tell people the gospel story, too?

One of the first pastors to have a radio program was Warren C. Roark in Canton, Ohio. He broadcast a half-hour program of music and inspirational messages from a station in nearby Akron. Many others shared Roark's belief in radio's power to spread the gospel of Jesus. By 1946 Church of God pastors were on forty-five different radio programs.

At this time the Board of Church Extension and Home Missions decided to sponsor one radio program that would be heard all across the United States.

Chapter 4:
Spreading the Word

They named this program the "Christian Brotherhood Hour," and its first broadcast took place in January, 1947. The speaker was a pastor from Park Place Church of God in Anderson, W. Dale Oldham. He served as the radio minister of the Church of God for more than twenty years. In 1968 he retired and R. Eugene Sterner took over as CBH speaker. Nine years later Sterner was followed by James Earl Massey.

People in the Church of God movement have always wanted to spread the gospel. In the early days of the movement the Flying Messengers, groups of evangelists, traveled by horse and wagon. Later they road the train. They used the great printing presses of the Gospel Trumpet Company to publish books, tracts, and the *Gospel Trumpet*. These, too, were ways that Church of God people could tell others about their experience in the Lord.

Speakers on the Christian Brotherhood Hour up to 1980 included Dale Oldham (top), Eugene Sterner (center), and James Massey (lower).

The Gospel Trumpet
Company was first
employed in the printing of
the paper, books, and small
pamphlets and tracts. But
because it was the pub-
lishing house for the
Church of God movement,
the company also printed
materials that Church of
God congregations needed.
Sunday school teachers
needed written materials
for their lessons each
Sunday. The Trumpet
Company printed these
materials for the church.

In 1931 A.T. Rowe
became the general
manager of the Gospel
Trumpet Company. He
stayed in that job until
1949. Some of the years
that he managed the
company were very difficult
because America was going
through the Great Depres-
sion. Many businesses
failed during the 1930s, but
Rowe worked hard to save
the Gospel Trumpet Com-
pany. Sometimes he had to
make unpopular decisions.
Rowe reduced the hours of
some men and women who
worked at the company to
only two or three days a
week. Sometimes they were
laid off and did not work at
all. Some people criticized
Rowe and said he was a
cold, heartless man. He was

stung by this criticism but nevertheless stayed at his job. The Gospel Trumpet Company came through the depression, in large part, thanks to the courage and determination of people like A.T. Rowe.

At the same time that Rowe became general manager, the *Gospel Trumpet* got a new editor. His name was Charles E. Brown. For several years Brown had been the pastor of a congregation in Detroit, Michigan. He took the editor's office at a time of deep disagreement between Anderson College President Morrison and the previous editor, F.G. Smith. Brown was a self-taught man with a great interest in the history of Christianity. While editor

The Gospel Trumpet Company has undergone many changes since 1930. Its name has been changed to Warner Press and the building occupied by the company has been remodeled several times. In the years since 1930 three men have served as Editor-in-Chief: Charles Brown (shown at his desk), Arlo Newell (lower left), and Harold Phillips (lower right).

he wrote many books, including *The Meaning of Salvation, The Church Beyond Division,* and *A New Approach to Christian Unity.*

C.E. Brown served as editor longer than any one before him. He retired in 1951, after twenty years as head of the editorial department. Editors who followed after C.E. Brown were Harold L. Phillips (1951-1977) and Arlo F. Newell (1977-). In the 1960s the magazine's name was changed from the *Gospel Trumpet* to *Vital Christianity* and the Gospel Trumpet Company's name was changed to Warner Press. But the concern of the editorial staff remained the same: to spread the news of what God has done.

In 1953 the Church of God General Ministerial Assembly decided that it needed a special group of people to think of ways that the Church of God could use new forms of communication—such as

Pictured above are members of the 1934 Editorial staff: (left to right), Burgess McCreary, Marvin Brown, Charles Brown, Alvina Koglin, and Helen Percy.

radio and television. So it created the Radio and Television Commission to coordinate these activities. In 1976 this commission became the Mass Communications Board and a year later Maurice Berquist was named its first executive-secretary. This board sponsored a television special called "The Doctor Is In" that was viewed by millions.

The people of the Church of God have tried to spread the word of the gospel in other ways. The year 1950 was the half-way year of the twentieth century. Just before that year a group of the movement's leaders came together to plan for a "Mid-Century Evangelistic Advance." They targeted

all aspects of the church's life for a renewed emphasis on evangelism under the slogan, "Go—Make Disciples."

One other way in which Church of God people have attempted to spread the gospel word is through music. Church of God people wrote hundreds of songs in the early days of the movement. People like Charles Naylor, Lawrence Brooks, D.S. Warner, D.O. Teasley and, especially, Barney E. Warren composed songs and lyrics that told of how wonderful it was to be saved from sin and become a child of God. They wrote of how precious was the love of Jesus that bound Christian hearts together.

With the coming of radio

and the recording industry, Church of God singers and musicians began performing songs as well as writing them. Trios and quartets had traveled for Church of God colleges since the 1930s. But the most famous of these musical spreaders of the word in the 1950s was the Christian Brothers Quartet. Paul Clausen, Ernie Gross, Doug Oldham, and Ron Patty warmed the hearts of thousands with their music and testimonies. In the late 1960s and early 1970s Bill and Gloria Gaither, Church of God laypersons from Alexandria, Indiana began composing and performing gospel songs of such quality and vitality that they became award-winning leaders in the gospel music industry. They, too, sought to spread the Word. □

The top photo shows people gathered around the Christian Brotherhood Hour building on the campground at Anderson.

Songwriter Barney Warren.

The original members of the Christian Brothers Quartet. Left to right: Doug Oldham, Ron Patty, Paul Clausen, and Ernie Gross. Pictured in the insert is Paul Yerden, accompanist for the group.

The Gaither Trio: Danny (standing), Gloria, and Bill.

*I*n the years from 1880 to 1930 Church of God people began many different kinds of church work. Many people started new churches and became pastors. Some started Sunday schools. (In the early days they were called "Sabbath schools.") Other people left the United States and traveled to foreign countries where they served as missionaries. Others worked in the United States as home missionaries. Still others joined in the work of Bible institutes and colleges.

During those early years, people in the Church of God movement were very much against the idea of organizing the church. They believed that since the church belonged to God, men and women should not try to organize it according to their ideas. Instead, they should let God organize the church through the gifts of the Holy Spirit. The people who were gifted to be preachers should preach. Those who were gifted to be helpers should help. Those who were gifted to be missionaries should serve. In this way God was thought to organize the

Chapter 5:
Organizing the Work

church. And so men and women of the Church of God movement started many different programs, which they often simply called *works*, "as the Lord led," they said.

Before long, however, people began to realize that a little more planning and guidance were needed in order to start new works. Some people didn't think that it was a good idea for lots of home missionaries to be working in one part of the United States and nobody working in another

part of the country.

Similarly, not all foreign missionaries should go to British East Africa while none went to Australia. Other people thought that Sunday school teachers should be given better lessons to teach and guidance on how to organize a Sunday school. Ministers began to think that it would be a good idea for them to meet once a year to discuss matters important to the life of the Church of God movement.

So it was that the need

for planning, guidance, and oversight led to the development of a whole host of boards, committees, and assemblies. By 1930 each of the following had been created:
General Ministerial Assembly (1917)
Anderson College (1917)
Missionary Board (1917)
National Association of the

In 1947 World Service Budget hoped to raise more than a million dollars for Church of God projects around the world.

Church of God (1917)
National Association
General Ministerial
Assembly (1917)
Board of Church Extension
and Home Missions (1920)
Board of Religious
Education and Sunday
Schools (1923)

In these same years the
Gospel Trumpet Company
became one of the general
agencies of the Church of
God movement as well.
The development of so
many boards and planning
groups gave many people
in the Church of God an
uneasy conscience. They
perceived that, in spite of
our deep convictions
against organization, that
was exactly what we had
done. About that time,
Charles E. Brown, who had
become the editor of the
Gospel Trumpet in 1930,
said that the new boards
and committees had not
organized the church itself.
They had instead organized

Directors of the Division of World Service up to 1980 have included C.W. Hatch (above) and Paul Tanner (below), who left that office to become Executive Secretary of the Executive Council of the Church of God.

the work that the church was to carry out.

Even after Brown solved the problem of whether all the new organization was good, problems remained. One of the biggest of those problems was money. Each of the boards or "agencies" needed money to carry out its work. Foreign missionaries needed money to build churches and to purchase materials to help them share the gospel. The Board of Church Extension and Home Missions needed money to assist in the development of new congregations and to support home missionaries in their work among Hispanics, native Americans, and others. Colleges needed money to buy books for libraries and to pay the salaries of professors and others who worked there. Where would money come from to meet all these needs?

Each of the agencies looked to the individual congregations for the financial support it needed. That meant that people from the agencies spent a great deal of time traveling around the United States, appealing to people in Church of God congregations for offerings to support their work. This practice was not very systematic or efficient. Congregations became weary of repeated requests for money coming from various agency representatives, each person asking money for his or her own specific work.

In 1930 it was also true that Church of God people were not yet accustomed to the idea of regularly giving money for church work, a practice called tithing. A person who tithes gives one tenth of her or his income to the church. Lots of early Church of God preachers attacked what they called the "tithe system." It wasn't that they did not think people should give to the work of the church, for these preachers believed that God is the real owner of everything anyway. But they also thought that tithing worked an unfair hardship on the poor and discouraged the rich from being as generous as they could and should be.

Another reason why Church of God people were unfamiliar with the practice of tithing is that in the early days many of them were farmers or rural people who raised much of what they needed for food and the other necessities of life. So they didn't have or need a great deal of money to live. They were accustomed to giving to preachers and gospel workers. But their gifts often took the form of the goods they produced. So instead of paying the preacher in money so that he or she could buy groceries for the family, Church of God people in those early days might bring a ham, some fruit or vegetables from their gardens, maybe some milk or butter from the family's dairy cow, or a couple of live chickens. They might also bring the preacher a coat that someone had outgrown or a wagon load of wood to burn for heating during the winter. But especially after 1930 these forms of giving were exchanged for the new (in the Church of God) practice of tithing.

In 1927 the five agencies (Missionary Board, Church Extension, Sunday School, Gospel Trumpet Company, and Anderson College) agreed on a new plan of fund-raising for their work. Instead of working independently of each other, they decided to plan their budgets and submit them

34

to a committee of the General Ministerial Assembly. This committee would decide what the final budget of each agency would be. Fund-raising was to be done in cooperation with each other, rather than separately. So was created what became known as the "Associated Budgets."

In 1941 the Associated Budgets became "World Service," which later became one of the divisions of the Executive Council of the General Assembly. The World Service division is the fund-raising arm of the Church of God movement. Each year it assists the budget committee of the General Assembly in planning out the requests

Since 1917 black Church of God congregations and ministers have been organized as the National Association of the Church of God and the General Assembly of that same association. Among the several outstanding leaders of that fellowship have been Raymond Jackson (top), Marcus Morgan (center left), Lawrence Wyatt (center right), and Robert Culp.

*Executive Council
Executive Secretaries
Charles V. Weber (above)
and William E. Reed.*

that come from the several church divisions, commissions, and agencies. A budget is prepared, and the World Service staff assists congregations in raising the money to meet this budget, which then is used to support Church of God projects around the world. In 1950 the World Service budget was $800,000. By 1980 the budget had grown to $7,040,500.

Over the years since 1930 the work of the agencies and commissions of the General Assembly has continued growing. New agencies have been added: Gulf-Coast Bible College (later renamed Mid-America Bible College), Mass Communications Board, Pensions Board, and Warner Pacific College. Commissions also were created to deal with the important issues of Christian unity, higher education, and social concerns. And the divisions of World Service, General Service, and Church Service assist in the day-to-day conduct of church business. All of these agencies, commissions, and divisions have specific assignments that are part of the organized work of the Church of God. □

Chapter 6:
Christian Education

The idea of going to Sunday school may be very familiar to you today, and the majority of Church of God congregations now have Sunday school programs. But in the very first years of the Church of God movement this was not so. Many leaders thought that Sunday schools were a bad idea. Some felt that God did not want churches to have Sunday schools. Others had the idea that Sunday schools did not help children to follow Jesus faithfully.

In spite of these feelings, D.S. Warner and others were concerned that children learn the teachings of the Bible. Gradually these people decided that strictly controlled Sunday schools could be allowed. Church of God people liked this change of mind. In 1911 D.O. Teasley wrote a book that explained to local church leaders how to conduct a Sunday school. By 1923 about five hundred such schools had been organized in Church of God congregations across America.

The year 1923 was very important in Church of

God Christian education. In June of that year, the General Ministerial Assembly created a new board to assist the growing Sunday school work. This group was called the Board of Religious Education and Sunday Schools. Many people simply called it the "Sunday school board." Four years later Bessie Hittle Byrum became president of the Board, and then its importance grew even more rapidly.

The Board's work covered all phases of Christian education: Sunday schools, vacation

Christian education in the Church of God has required dedicated writers and editors of Sunday school and other educational materials. Kenneth Hall, shown in the lower photo, served many years as the editor of adult curriculum at Warner Press. Leaders in the work of the church's educational ministry have included Donald Courtney (upper right) and T. Franklin Miller (center), who both served as Executive Secretary-Treasurer of the Board of Christian Education, and long-time curriculum editor and writer, Lottie Franklin.

Bible school, curriculum, youth work, and teacher training programs. Always, however, students mattered most to Bessie Byrum. She taught Sunday school teachers to think of their classes as small churches in which each class member was important. She thought that Sunday schools offered the greatest opportunity for the church to grow. For forty years she also served as the superintendent of Sunday school at Park Place Church of God in Anderson, Indiana. She also got the church to try some new ideas; for example, she got her church to try a vacation

Youth conventions have been part of life in the Church of God for a long time and among several ethnic groups. The top photograph shows delegates to the first Hispanic youth convention, held in Anderson in 1978. The lower two photos show scenes from the Inspirational Youth Convention held at St. Louis in 1980. A gathering of delegates at one of the early young people's conventions at Anderson is shown in the center photo.

Bible school for the first time.

In 1929 Church of God young people voted to begin their own International Youth Convention at a time and place other than at Anderson Camp Meeting. The youth work of the Church of God also was the responsibility of the Sunday school board. But not until 1946 did the Board assume responsibility for planning the convention. The first young people's convention was held at the 1924 Anderson Camp Meeting. One day of the general camp meeting emphasized the young people of the movement.

In addition to holding conventions such as the one pictured above, youth work in the Church of God has involved international work camps and conventions. Such an event occurred at Fritzlar, West Germany, in 1955. American delegates are shown on board the ship which carried them across the Atlantic Ocean. Pictured below are Christian education leaders in the Church of God (left to right) Betty Jo Hutchison, Ronald Fowler, Donald Courtney, Arlo Newell, and Irene Caldwell.

After the separation of the young people's convention from the general camp meeting, the youth work took on greater and greater importance.

The first separate convention of young people met in South Bend, Indiana under the theme "Making the World Christian." About 190 delegates attended. Over the years youth convention attendance grew dramatically. Nearly 6,000 delegates came to Louisville for the 1964 convention, the largest convention of Church of God young people ever.

The International Youth Convention is held in even-numbered years. One interesting feature of the convention is that the age of delegates is now younger than in the early years. Then, young adults were still considered "youth." Men such as Russell Olt and Adam Miller, already actively involved in full-time ministry, served as convention presidents from 1930 to 1948. (Olt became the dean of Anderson College in 1925 and Miller had already been a missionary in Japan.) The convention in later years has been attended primarily by high school freshmen through seniors.

Youth conventions became great rallying times for the church's young people. Inspirational services combined with informative and helpful conferences make exciting meetings. Every other year Church of God youth have gathered in such cities as San Diego, Edmonton, Louisville, Philadelphia, Miami, and Minneapolis. Until 1970, the campaigns and elections of the convention officers were features of the convention. In association with others these officers were

responsible for planning the next convention. Among these elected presidents of the convention were Russell Olt, Adam Miller, Dondeena Fleenor, Norman Beard, and Marcia Guttenfelder. James Cook was the last convention president, elected in 1970. In 1972 international convention officers were replaced by a national planning council made up of seven regional representatives.

Leaders in the National Association of the Church of God also felt the need for a meeting designed especially for young people. Pansie Brown, Josie Greer, and Ruth Keith had hoped that youth could be given responsibility for leading a whole day of activities at the West Middlesex Camp Meeting. In the 1920s one day of the meeting was set aside as Youth Day; young people preached, led singing, and generally were in charge of the day's worship services.

Out of this experience grew the idea of an Inspirational Youth Convention led by officers of a national youth fellowship. Ted Armstead, Josie Greer, and Gabriel Dixon were the first three presidents of this youth fellowship. Dixon had the idea that the best time for a convention would be right after Christmas. Plans for the convention were made and the announcements were sent out. Delegates numbering about six hundred attended the first Inspirational Youth Convention, held in Chicago in December, 1938. Over the years the convention has grown in attendance until now more than four thousand delegates participate in the annual meeting.

In addition to Gabriel Dixon, other noted leaders of the Church of God who have served as presidents of this convention are Dr. James E. Massey, Rev. Robert Culp, Dr. Edward Foggs, and Dr. Ronald Fowler. □

Chapter 7:
Schools

B etween 1910 and 1920 Church of God people started four different Bible institutes. These were schools in which men and women took courses to help them learn how to preach, to lead singing, and to teach. These schools were located in Kansas City; Anderson, Indiana; Spokane, Washington; and New York City. The Bible training school in Anderson grew to become Anderson College and Theological Seminary in 1925. The Kansas City school soon closed. So did the institutions at New York and Spokane, but not before important ground was laid for future schools.

The New York institute was part of the missionary home in that city. Its leader was D.O. Teasley. He and his friends, George Tasker and A.D. Khan, together wrote a correspondence course for ministerial students. Those who lived far from New York could therefore study by taking courses through the mail. One of the young people who took the correspond-ence study course was A.F. Gray.

A.F. Gray was born on a

farm near Grand Forks, North Dakota. His father died when Gray was still a young boy. So his mother moved her family to eastern Washington. They already knew about the Church of God from the years they attended the Grand Forks Camp Meeting. In these surroundings young Albert had felt the Spirit of God calling him to the ministry. To prepare himself for this work, Albert took practical training in the Spokane Institute and the New York correspondence course.

Over the years the Church of God movement respected Gray and his work more and more. He wrote an important textbook on theology. He chaired the General Ministerial Assembly of the Church of God for more than a decade. He was president of the Missionary Board, too. Gray also served as a trustee of Anderson College, but he believed that students in the Pacific Northwest

The seal of Mid-America Bible College, formerly Gulf-Coast Bible College and its two presidents Max Gaulke (lower left) and John Conley.

should also have a school. The old Spokane Institute had closed in the 1920s. In 1937 Gray and others believed that the time had come to make a new beginning. That year Pacific Bible College opened its doors for the first time. In its first year the school had only two teachers. One was President Gray, who still pastored the Woodland Park Church of God in Seattle. This meant that he was in Seattle on weekends, on the train Mondays and Fridays, and teaching Tuesday, Wednesday, and Thursday in Spokane. The other faculty member was Daisy Maiden Boone, a

The photo above shows Linn Library on the campus of Warner Pacific College, formerly Pacific Bible College. Traditionally, Church of God colleges have sponsored musical groups that toured the United States and Canada during summer vacation. Pictured below is one of the groups that represented Arlington College in the early 1960s. From left to right: Steve Merica, Martin Shackleton, accompanist Jean Helbling, Dale Fillmore, and Yoshihiro Uehara.

missionary to China, home for an extended furlough. She taught on Mondays and Fridays.

Pacific Bible College moved to Portland, Oregon in 1940. About the same time Dr. Otto F. Linn, the first minister in the Church of God to hold the academic degree Doctor of Philosophy, became the infant college's new dean. Together he and President Gray laid the foundations of a Christian liberal arts college. In 1959 Pacific Bible changed its name to Warner Pacific College.

During the depression of the 1930s and the years of World War II, shortages of money, food, gasoline, and other goods were common. Schools like Pacific Bible and Anderson College depended upon people to give money so they could continue to operate. Often Church of God people had

Warner Pacific College President A.F. Gray stands in front of the goods gathered during the college's annual Harvest Ingathering. Pictured below is Milo Chapman, veteran servant of Church of God higher education institutions at Arlington and Warner Pacific.

little or no money to give the colleges. But people still loved the schools and knew their importance to the church and its young people. Instead of money, people often gave food to the colleges for the student cafeteria. A young man named Bill Dudgeon used to drive the Anderson College truck through Indiana and Ohio, picking up loads of potatoes, carrots, green beans, and other vegetables and fruit that people gave the college. At Pacific Bible College the school held an annual Harvest Ingathering where people gave fresh and canned fruit, thousands of pounds of potatoes, sides of bacon, and, one year, two deer that had been shot by hunters from the Church of God in Twin Falls, Idaho.

Anderson College began as a Bible training school. J.T. Wilson, general manager of the Gospel Trumpet Company, had thought of the idea of a school in Anderson. He left Anderson in the 1920s and became the first president of a new Church of God college in Eastland, Texas in 1929. This school was named Warner Memorial University. But Wilson and the faculty at the new school were beginning just at the time of the Great Depression. Financial hard times forced the school to close after only a few years.

The closing of Warner Memorial University did not discourage others from beginning colleges. Two colleges and a seminary started in the early 1950s. In 1953 some ministers in southern California founded Arlington Bible College near Los Angeles. In 1968 Arlington merged with Azusa Pacific College. People in Texas also started a Bible college in 1953. South Texas Bible Institute opened its doors in Houston in 1953. Max Gaulke was its first president.

South Texas Bible Institute changed its name to Gulf-Coast Bible College in 1955. That same year its curriculum was expanded to a four-year program. Dr. Gaulke served as president until his retirement in 1975, when he was succeeded by John Conley.

In 1950 Anderson College opened the graduate School of Theology. This was a special, advanced school for the preparation of ministers. Earl L. Martin was the seminary's first dean. By 1955 some seventy-five students enrolled at the School of Theology.

Another college developed in the 1950s. The idea for this school grew in the mind of J. Horace Germany, a Church of God minister in Muncie, Indiana. Germany had grown up in Mississippi and was concerned about the poor educational opportunities for black people in that state. Most of all he wanted to help young black men and women prepare to be Church of God ministers. Just as his dream began coming true, Germany's school was shut down by racists. But Horace Germany refused to lay aside his dream. In 1961, the school opened at Kendleton, Texas. It was given the name Bay Ridge Christian College sponsored by the Southern Association of the Church of God. Bay Ridge has taken the special mission of training Church of God minority students for the ministry.

The Southeastern Asso-

ciation of the Church of God also opened a college in the 1960s. Concerned to provide a college near home for the region's young people, the Association voted to open Warner Southern College at Lake Wales, Florida. Leroy M. Fulton was Warner Southern's first president when classes began in 1968.

Unlike the other colleges of the Church of God, Warner Southern began as a liberal arts college. From the beginning its leaders intended to offer courses and programs of study for young men and women who were not planning to be ministers. Although people could study to be ministers at Warner Southern, the college wanted to offer the opportunity for all Christian young people to study there.

Before A.F. Gray and others started Pacific Bible

Horace Germany, founding president of Bay Ridge Christian College is shown above. Below are (left) Leroy Fulton, founding president of Warner Southern College, and Robert Nicholson, long-time Dean of Anderson University, who became the institution's third president.

College, Church of God ministers in Canada also felt the need for a Bible school. Harry C. Gardner led a group of concerned people into planning such a school, which opened in 1933 as Alberta Bible Institute. Dr. Gardner served as president of the school located in Camrose until 1953. In 1981 it was renamed Gardner Bible College in his honor. Unlike the other liberal arts Church of God colleges, Gardner has remained a Bible college and has focused its attention on the study of Bible and Christian education.

By the time the Church of God celebrated its one hundredth birthday in 1980, the movement had started at least a dozen schools of one sort or another. Although their programs of study have varied widely, these colleges have been united in the common goal of educating men and women who would become the kind of people who put their learning to use in the service of God and their fellow human beings. □

Pictured below is Robert Reardon, president of Anderson University from 1958 to 1983. The men in the other photos are the first deans of the graduate School of Theology, Earl Martin (upper left), Adam Miller (right) and Gene Newberry (center).

Conclusion

U nless you have skipped all the interesting stories and pictures that the previous chapters contain, you have now read about and seen photos of a great host of people, places, and enterprises connected with the Church of God movement. You've read the story of Nora Hunter and the Women of the Church of God. You've seen photos of Bill and Gloria Gaither and the Christian Brothers Quartet. You've read about the deep commitment and courage of early Church of God missionaries in British East Africa. Now it is time to ask the question, Why is it important to know all this, anyway?

In Deuteronomy 6 we read about a child who wants to know the meaning of the customs and ceremonies kept by the Israelites. The child's parents are instructed to answer this question by telling a story. This is no idle tale they are to tell, but the great story of the Exodus, God's miraculous delivery of Israel from Egyptian slavery. The stories you have read here are not nearly so dramatic or grand as the story of the Exodus. But just as the child who asks questions about Israel's belief and practices, we, too, need to know the meaning of those things that help to make us part of the Church of God movement. Without such stories, the way we worship, the ministries to which we give our money, and many other things begin to lose their importance in our eyes. When that happens, we, too, begin to lose our way, because those stories also help us keep our bearings as we journey through life.

So while the stories of the Church of God are not as well-known or dramatic as the stories of the Bible, certainly, nor perhaps those of other church groups either, that does not mean that these stories are not important or useful. For they contain lessons about commitment and sacrifice to a particular vision of the church. That vision is one of the points on the compass by which we in the Church of God seek to steer our lives. That vision was sought by our Lord and Master himself when he prayed for his followers "that they all might be one."